Ropers and Riders

Josepha Sherman

Heinemann Library
Chicago, Illinois

Customer Service 888-454-2279

Designed by Lisa Buckley
Printed in Hong Kong

04 03 02 01 00
10 9 8 7 6 5 4 3 2 1

Library of Congress Cataloging-in-Publication Data
Sherman, Josepha.
    Ropers and riders / Josepha Sherman.
        p. cm. – (Rodeo)
    Includes bibliographical references (p.) and index.
    Summary: Describes the origins, training, and techniques of calf roping, as well as animals and gear used, judging the event at a rodeo, and more.
        ISBN 1-57572-506-1 (lib. bdg.)
        1. Rodeos—Juvenile literature. 2. Rodeo performers—Juvenile literature. [1. Calf roping. 2. Rodeos.] I. Title.

GV1834.S54 2000
791.8'4—dc21
                                                99-048967

Acknowledgments
The author and publishers are grateful to the following for permission to reproduce copyright material:
Steve Bly, pp. 4, 6, 8, 12, 14, 16, 20, 25; The Granger Collection, p. 5; Ben Klaffke, pp. 7, 10, 11; Dudley Barker, pp. 9, 19; Jack Upton, pp. 13, 28; Photo 20-20, p. 15; AP/Wide World p. 17; Dan Hubbell, pp. 18, 22, 27; Erwin C. "Bud" Nielsen/Images International, p. 21; George D. Lepp/Photo Researchers, p. 23; Jerry Wachter/Photo Researchers, p. 24.

Cover photograph: Steve Bly

Special thanks to Dan Sullivan of the Calgary Stampede for his comments in the preparation of this book.

Every effort has been made to contact copyright holders of any material reproduced in this book.
Any omissions will be rectified in subsequent printings if notice is given to the publisher.

Some words are shown in bold, **like this.**
You can find out what they mean by looking in the glossary.

Contents

On the Ranch, Then and Now

A cowboy keeps the cattle moving on a roundup.

The cowboy sits on his horse, looking over the herd of **cattle**. They look like a slowly moving sea of brown. In that herd is one small calf that needs medicine, and another that must be marked with the ranch brand. How can the cowboy catch the calves without frightening the whole herd?

In the 1800s, the best way for a cowboy to catch a calf was to ride his horse quietly into the herd and then rope the calf. And that's still the best way to do it. A horse moving quietly through a herd is less scary to the cattle than today's truck or helicopter. And a skillfully thrown rope is still the quickest, safest way to catch a calf.

Long ago, cowboys began competing to see who was the best calf roper. This makes calf roping one of the oldest events in the sport of rodeo.

A ranch has other roping jobs, too. Sometimes a cowboy has to rope a full-grown **steer**. But some steers are too large or dangerous for one cowboy to handle. So two cowboys rope a steer by its horns and hind legs so that it can't get away or hurt them or their horses. This is called team roping, and it is also a rodeo event.

A cowboy "cuts" a calf out of the herd.

What Is Calf Roping?

A roper and his horse chase a calf, ready to rope it. The cowboy holds the **piggin' string** between his teeth.

Calf roping is a fast-paced and exciting event that gets a rodeo crowd cheering. It shows off the teamwork of horse and rider. It demonstrates the cowboy's skill.

A calf speeds out of a **chute**, getting a 12 foot (3.5 meter) head start. As it runs, it breaks a rope barrier, starting the timer. The cowboy and his horse take off after the calf in the split second after it breaks the barrier. If he starts too soon, there's a ten-second penalty. If he starts too late, the calf has too much of a head start.

As the cowboy and his horse overtake the calf, the cowboy throws his rope. The only **legal catch**, also called a **fair catch**, is around the calf's neck. A cowboy gets two tries, but if he misses the first time, he's probably **"out of the money."**

Once the calf is caught, the cowboy quickly takes a **dally** around the saddle's **horn**, looping the end of the rope around it. His horse keeps the rope between the calf and the saddle tight as the cowboy races to the calf and throws it on its side to the ground. If the calf fell down when it was roped, the cowboy must get it to its feet and then throw it. The calf roper uses the 6 foot (2 meter) piggin' string that he carries between his teeth to tie three of the calf's feet. The piggin' string is secured with a knot called a **hooey,** or **half-hitch**. The cowboy throws his hands into the air to signal the finish, and the timer is stopped. The tie must hold the calf for another six seconds, or the cowboy is disqualified. The fastest time wins.

As the cowboy catches the calf, his horse goes back on its **haunches.** The cowboy is about to leap off.

Training the Calf Roper

Some calf ropers start their careers as ranch children growing up around cowboys. They often help the cowboys with ranch work such as herding **cattle**. They also learn the basic skills of riding and roping from the moment they can first sit in the saddle.

Other calf ropers begin their rodeo careers in children's roping events that include boys and girls from eight to eighteen years old. But there's no rule about when a child can start practicing. Even children under the age of five can try roping a dummy calf. These very young ropers start off roping on foot. Older boys, from about ten years of age and into their teens, can try roping dummy calves and then live ones from horseback.

A boy learns how to rope. He's starting by making a loop.

This young rider has made a **fair catch** by roping the calf's head.

Cowboys can learn roping as adults, too. There are schools that teach roping from the backs of experienced, patient horses. The beginning roper, however, quickly finds that it's not too easy to rope anything and all too easy to do something silly, such as hitting his horse in an ear with the rope. At first, the only targets a learning roper uses are dummy calves. But when his skill increases, he can begin roping live animals. When he can rope a live calf at a full **gallop,** he's ready for the rodeo.

The Horse

Anyone watching calf roping will be impressed with the skill of the roper and just as impressed with the skill of the horse. A good roping horse knows exactly what to do. It races out of the **chute** and brings the cowboy within roping reach of the running calf. As soon as the cowboy throws his rope, the horse pulls back on its **haunches** to tighten the rope and to keep the calf from wriggling loose. The horse then watches the calf, backing up if necessary to keep the rope tight.

As the cowboy ties the calf, the horse takes a step back to keep the rope tight.

The horse will not move until the cowboy gets in the saddle.

How is a horse trained? Certain horses, particularly those from breeds such as the **American quarter horse,** are said to have **cow sense** and a love of herding **cattle**. Such horses quickly learn how to close in on a running calf. They learn from practice and rewards that the point of the game is to keep the calf from escaping by holding the rope tight. A good roping horse seems to enjoy its work.

The Calf

There are some people who think that calf roping is cruel. They say that it hurts or frightens it. But there are rules protecting the rodeo calves, just as there are rules protecting all the other animals.

Calves may be young animals, but they aren't that small. They aren't really soft and weak, either. By rodeo rules, a calf used in roping must weigh at least 200 pounds (91 kilograms) and it may weigh more. A calf's ribs are so tough that a cowboy who accidentally kicks one during the event can bruise or break a toe.

A cowboy can be fined if he treats a rodeo calf roughly.

There are also rules about the way in which a calf may be roped. A calf cannot be caught so violently that it is **jerked down** or flipped over onto its back. In fact, a cowboy can be penalized for too rough of a catch.

Calves aren't trained to run. That comes naturally to them. There's no way to predict what they'll do, either. Some run in a nice, straight line. Others dash about or start kicking or bucking. This makes it very difficult for a cowboy to rope them. But the calf a cowboy gets is the luck of the draw.

Some of the best athletes in rodeo are calf ropers.

What Is Team Roping?

Team roping, like calf roping, comes straight out of ranch work. It is the only official rodeo event that is done as a team. Team roping is a partnership of two riders, the **team header** and the **team heeler**, and their two horses. This sport uses a **steer** instead of a calf.

The team roping event begins when the steer is let out of its **chute** and goes racing across the arena. The header starts the timer as he and his horse speed out of their chute in pursuit. The header is the one who makes the quick decisions and directs the play. He must rope the steer by the horns and turn it away from the heeler, who is coming up from behind.

Team ropers chase a steer. The header is roping this steer's horns.

These team ropers have almost made a **fair catch**. The header has roped the steer's horns, but the heeler has roped only one hind leg.

The heeler's job isn't any easier. He must rope the steer by both hind legs. There is a five-second penalty if the heeler catches only one leg. Once the steer is securely caught, with both horses holding the ropes tight, the timer is stopped.

Training the
Team Ropers

How do team ropers get started? If the team is to be a success, each member of the team must be a skilled roper. He or she may have learned those roping skills growing up on a ranch, practicing in children's rodeo events, or in a roping school.

Another important aspect of team roping is having trust in each other. Each of the two cowboys must depend on the other to do his or her part of the event. And each must understand that no one is perfect. Even the best roper can have an off day.

This boy already shows good riding style.

Beginning ropers learn by practicing with dummy steers.

To work well as a team, the two cowboys must practice as a team. There are schools for this training, too. There are even computerized models of **steers** on which they can fine tune their teamwork. And of course, the best way to learn how to work as a team is to try roping live steers.

A team can start small with the smaller rodeos. Then, as they begin to gather wins, the team ropers can move on to the professional rodeos.

The Steer

Team roping is another of the rodeo events that angers some people. They see the quick action and the **steer** caught between two ropes. They are afraid that the steer is going to get hurt.

What these people don't always know is that a steer is a fully grown animal. It is even stronger and tougher than a calf. In rodeos, each steer must weigh at least 500 hundred pounds (227 kilograms), and usually it weighs a great deal more. During the team roping event, the steer isn't jerked off its feet or thrown down in any way. Great care is taken to make sure it isn't hurt by the ropes.

On the ranch, cowboys roped steers in order to give them medical care.

An animal that isn't healthy won't put on a good show.
Stock contractors take very good care of their rodeo animals.

In fact, there are rules to watch over a steer's health, just as there are for all the other animals in the rodeo. A veterinarian is always on duty. He or she is the doctor who checks each steer before and after every rodeo. The veterinarian makes certain that each animal is healthy and hasn't gotten hurt. And a steer may not be overworked at the rodeo, either. A rodeo steer is given plenty of rest time, good food, and clean living conditions.

Women in Roping

In ranch work, women sometimes rope calves alongside the men. Up until the 1930s, women also competed in calf roping events. But rodeo officials decided that most rodeo sports were too dangerous for women. They limited women's appearances to barrel racing and a few other safer events.

One event for women ropers is called breakaway calf roping. This event is adapted from traditional calf roping and begins the same way. But a woman isn't required to throw or tie the calf, merely to rope it. The rope is tied to the saddle **horn** with a piece of string. The rope pops free when the running calf is roped. A handkerchief tied to the rope serves as a flag that tells when the rope has broken free. This marks the contestant's time.

This cowgirl is about to rope her calf in the event called breakaway calf roping.

Another sport in which girls participate is called goat tying. In this event, a goat is tethered at one end of the arena. The contestant rides at a **gallop** from the other end of the arena, crosses a starting line, and starts the time clock. Dismounting at a run, she grabs the goat, which is doing its best to squirm away. She throws it down and ties three of its legs with her **piggin' string**. She signals time by throwing up her hands. The goat has to stay tied for five more seconds. As with calf roping, the fastest time wins.

A goat weighs much less than a calf and is a little easier to tie.

Judging

The rodeo judges decide who has won each event. What do judges look for in **calf** roping and team roping? They're watching for the fastest times, which run between eight and twelve seconds for calf roping and around six seconds for team roping.

One thing that judges always want to see in calf roping is a **fair catch**. There cannot be any unnecessary roughness towards the calf. The catching, throwing, and tying must be done right. And the judges time those all-important six seconds that a calf must remain tied if a cowboy's score is to count.

Team ropers have to be careful, too. The **team heeler** can't rope the **steer's** hind legs until the **team header** has turned the steer in the right direction. And only the right targets, horns for the header and both hind feet for the heeler, can be legally roped.

Judges keep a careful eye on roping events to make sure the rules are being followed.

If the calf doesn't stay roped for six seconds after the cowboy ties it, the cowboy will get no time for all his hard work.

But even when a cowboy has successfully roped a calf or steer, that doesn't mean he's won a roping event. There are several rounds for each event, as many as ten. This means that each calf roper has to successfully catch ten calves, and each roping team has to successfully catch ten steers. The judges keep track of the times for each round. It's the calf roper or roping team with the best overall time who finally wins.

Roping Gear

In the early days of rodeo, a calf rope was made of carefully braided leather. Nowadays, a calf or team rope is more likely to be made of a **synthetic** material, such as **polyester**, or a **nylon** and polyester blend. The same is true of the short **piggin' string**. This, too, is likely to be made of nylon.

Piggin' string   Calf rope

A roping horse is always outfitted in Western gear. It may wear a **bridle** with a **curb bit**, although good roping horses don't need too much guidance. Or it may have a hackamore, a type of bitless bridle. A horse wearing a hackamore is guided by pressure placed on the long bone of its nose.

A roping horse also wears a roping saddle. This looks like the traditional Western saddle, but it has a strong **horn** in front and stronger **cinches** to resist the strain of roping and catching calves and **steers**.

Cinch   Horn   Bridle   Curb bit

Roping Stars

Cody Ohl

Calf roper Cody Ohl won two straight world championships in 1997 and 1998. Out of nine rounds of calf roping competition in 1998, he won four and finished second in one. He also won record earnings for calf roping in 1998 of $222,794.

Jeff Chapman

Jeff Chapman set a new time record in 1997 at the National Finals Rodeo by roping and tying a calf in 6.8 seconds.

Dean Oliver

Dean Oliver holds a record for the most world championship calf roping titles. He has eight that he earned in the 1960s. He also ties with Roy Cooper for the most consecutive world titles for calf roping. Oliver won his five consecutive world titles in the 1960s, and Cooper won his five in the 1980s.

Jim Rodriguez, Jr.

In 1959, Jim Rodriguez, Jr., became the youngest team roping champion ever at age 18.

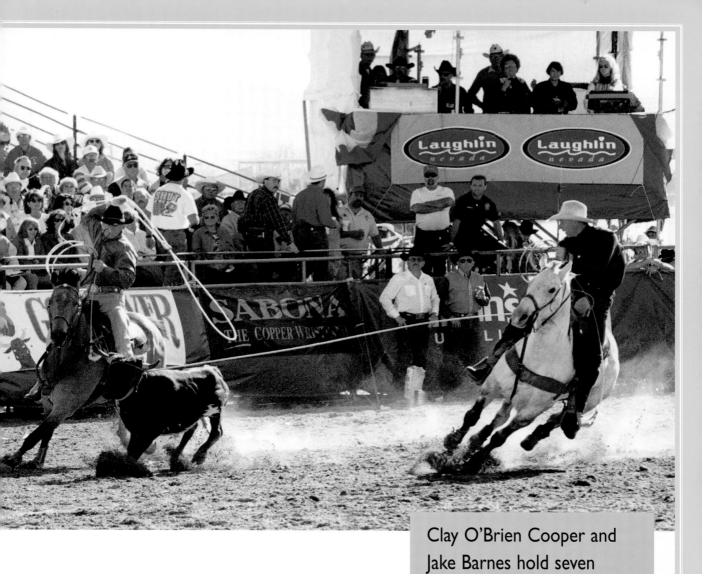

Clay O'Brien Cooper and Jake Barnes hold seven world championship team roping titles.

Clay O'Brien Cooper and Jake Barnes

Clay O'Brien Cooper and Jake Barnes hold the record for the most world championship team roping titles. They also hold the record for the most consecutive team roping championships. They have five, won from 1985 to 1989.

Associations

Montana Team Ropers
Association
P.O. Box 221
Huntley, Mont. 49037
(406) 967-2454

United States Team Roping
Championships
7511 Fourth Street NW
Albuquerque, N. Mex. 87107
(505) 897-9743

Roping and Riding Facts and Figures

Fastest Times on Record

Calf Roping

1978 Lee Phillips, Assiniboia, Saskatchewan   5.7 seconds

1986 Joe Beaver, West Jordan, Utah   6.7 seconds

1995 Cody Ohl, Billings, Montana   6.8 seconds

1997 Jeff Chapman, San Francisco   6.8 seconds

Team Roping

1986 Bob Harris and Tee Woolman, Spanish Fork, Utah
3.7 seconds

1983 Dee Pickett and Mike Beers, Abilene, Texas 3.8 seconds
tied with

1995 Doyle Gellerman and Britt Bockius, Las Vegas, Nevada
3.8 seconds
tied with

1998 Speed Williams and Rich Skelton, Las Vegas, Nevada
3.8 seconds

Glossary

American quarter horse   breed of horse often used in ranch and rodeo work that is known for its speed over short distances, its agility, and its intelligence

bridle   straps and metal pieces that fit on a horse's head and in its mouth

calf   baby cattle; more than one are called calves

cattle   cows, bulls, steers, and calves

chute   narrow holding pen that opens onto the rodeo arena

cinch   buckled strap that holds a saddle in place

cow sense   horse's love of herding cattle

curb bit   metal piece that fits in a horse's mouth, and that connects to the reins

dally   loop at the end of a rope around the saddle's horn

fair catch   in roping, catching a calf or steer by the proper target, such as the horns, neck, or hind legs; also known as a legal catch

gallop   fastest gait, or movement, of a horse

half-hitch   type of knot used in calf and steer roping to tie the calf or steer's legs; also called a hooey

haunches   hindquarters of an animal

horn   front of a western saddle that curves up to hold a rope

hooey   rodeo term for a half-hitch knot

jerked down   illegal move in which a calf or steer is roped so roughly that it is pulled over backwards

legal catch   another term for fair catch

nylon   strong type of plastic, often used in fabric or ropes

out of the money   not a winner

piggin' string   soft, six-foot (two meter) rope used to tie a calf or steer's legs; also called piggin or pigging

polyester   type of plastic, like nylon, often used in fabrics or ropes

steer   young adult male cattle that cannot reproduce

synthetic   any material not found in nature, such as plastic or nylon

team header   cowboy in team roping who starts the action by roping the steer by the horns

team heeler   cowboy in team roping who ropes the steer by the hind legs

More Books to Read

Gabbert, Lisa. *An American Rodeo: Riding & Roping*. New York: Rosen Publishing Group, 1998.

Gordon, Ginger. *Anthony Reynoso: Born to Rope*. New York: Houghton Mifflin Company, 1996.

Hoyt-Goldsmith, Diane. *Apache Rodeo*. New York: Holiday House, 1995.

Index